# THE GOLDEN AGE OF SHOP DESIGN:
## EUROPEAN SHOP INTERIORS 1880-1939

# THE GOLDEN AGE OF SHOP DESIGN:
## EUROPEAN SHOP INTERIORS 1880-1939

### EDITED BY ALEXANDRA ARTLEY

THE ARCHITECTURAL PRESS LONDON

*Photographic Acknowledgements*

**Figures refer to pages in which illustrations occur**

*National Monuments Record, London:* 2–3, 16–29, 32–37, 62–63, 72–73; *Novosti Press Agency:* 14–15; *Archives de l'Architecture Moderne, Brussels:* 30–31, 40–43, 44–45 left, 48–49 right, 50–53, 59, 64 right, 68–69, 78–79, 112–13 above and left, 114 below; *Bildarchiv Preussischer Kulturbesitz, Berlin:* 38–39, 64 above, 65–67, 70–71; *Courtesy of J. Sainsbury Ltd, London:* 45 above; *Staatsbibliothek, Berlin:* 47–48; *Courtesy of Express Dairy Ltd, Ruislip:* 48 top and above; *Courtesy of Harrods Ltd, London:* 54–55 left, 56–57, 108–111, 112 far left, 114–15 far right and bottom centre, 124 above right and centre; *Julian Barnard:* 55 above and top; *Gerlach:* 58 above; *Courtesy of The Architectural Review:* 58 right, 86–87, 102 above, 104–5, 114 right, 115 bottom right, 117–18 left, 125 far right, 127 left and above; *Kunstindustrimuseet, Copenhagen:* 60–61; *J. Pietrusinski:* 74–75; *The Architectural Press Ltd, London:* 76–77, 98 right, 99, 103, 106–7, 119 above, 122–23, 126–27 left; *Ernst Pollak Verlag, Berlin:* 80 top, 84–85 left, 88 top, 91, 92 right, 93 centre right; *Rijksbureau voor Kunsthistorische Documentatie, The Hague:* 80 centre right and right, 100–1, 102 right; *Chevojon:* 81, 83, 88 above, 88–89 right, 90, 92–93 above, 93 top right and bottom right; *Courtesy of the National Federation of Fish Friers, Leeds:* 82; *Royal Institute of British Architects, London:* 85, 98 below; *Courtesy of Westwood, Piet, Poole and Smart, London:* 94–97, 120–21; *Courtesy of Heal & Son Ltd, London:* 117 above and top, 118–19 left, top and right. Thanks are also due to *Bill Toomey* for invaluable photographic work.

**Previous page: children's toy bazaar at Charles Jenner & Company, Edinburgh in 1895**

ISBN: 0 85139 561 9
First Published 1975 by The Architectural Press Ltd
© The Architectural Press Ltd 1975
Designed by Rick Fawcett/Dark Design Studio

Printed in Great Britain by Jolly & Barber Ltd, Rugby

# CONTENTS

# INTRODUCTION

The thousands of shoppers who daily push back and forth through the plate glass doors of department stores in every major city in Europe, do so with the blasé assurance of building users who suppose that such commercial institutions have been there for their pleasure, convenience and ruin since time immemorial and will always continue to be there: an idea most impressively reinforced by the majestic and comforting late 19th- and early 20th-century solidity of fabric of the longest established companies. Yet, when compared with the churches, cathedrals, theatres, hotels and private residences which together form the cityscape to which we are accustomed, department stores, despite the dignified columnation of *fin-de-siècle* examples or the brilliant streamlined glamour of those built during the 1920s and '30s, are as building types merely vigorous infants demanding attention in the venerable family of buildings which constitutes the urban environment.

When one considers that the crowds who thronged under the brilliant lights of London's Gaiety Theatre, built by Norman Shaw and Ernest Runtz between 1902–03, were using a building which in its idea and the disposition of the public differed very little from that used by the crowds who sat under the Greek sun to watch the tragedies of Aeschylus, or that for all its dramatic showbiz technology Mission Control, Houston is in essence merely a new and appropriately late 20th-century version of Jenner's cowpox laboratory, it becomes clear that the department store, like the railway station, was a highly original and necessary building type given by 19th-century entrepreneurs and their architects to an astonished but receptive public.

In searching through European history for the moment when the department store was conceived, one finds that its putative parents are as usual dramatically ill-assorted. On the architectural side of the family, credit for the first design for a building which anticipates the form the department store was ultimately to take is given generally to the Neuruppin-born architect Karl Friedrich Schinkel (1781–1841) who during the 1820s produced designs for a shop in which the façades consisted of very large areas of glass divided by masonry piers. This idea so readily forecast the grid-iron, steel-framed façades of the next century, that Bruno Taut (1880–1938) one of the chief early 20th-century disseminators of glass as a major building material, reproduced Schinkel's design in his *Modern Architecture* published in 1929.[1]

Schinkel's designs for a prototype department store remained, however, on paper as a nameless prophesy and to infuse the aesthetic idea with the redder blood of commercial viability, it took the financial vision of the other side of the department store family, Madame and Monsieur Aristide Bouçicaut, two unparalleled virtuoso performers on the mid 19th-century Parisian cash register. The retail career of the Bouçicauts, which began in 1852, provides one of the more celebrated chapters in the traditional tale of commercial struggle and ultimate triumph which causes tears of pride to be forced back in centennial board-rooms everywhere. The well-loved story is that of The Retailer of Vision who, after vanquishing the monsters of bankruptcy, stock control and cash flow, moves in two generations from the rain-swept market stall or the lowly (but clean) side-street premises to his rightful apotheosis as the proprietor of a respected and fashionable emporium, outside which carriages can at last legitimately set down the mighty.

Although one thorough social historian of shopping in Britain feels that at least two, and possibly more, establishments were trading in the British provinces on departmental store principles before 1850, credit for pioneering modern methods of retailing is given generally to the Bon Marché of the Bouçicauts.[2] This may be because their innovations are better documented, or in their own day better advertised to the encouragement of imitators, or simply it may be that 19th-century Englishmen, ever fearful of 'trade', drew from the vigorous Bon Marché across the Channel the exquisite pleasure of contradicting Napoleon Bonaparte.

In 1852 the Bouçicauts opened a small shop on the unfashionable Parisian Left Bank for the sale of piece-goods which may be defined as fabrics manufactured in standard lengths.[3] Gradually they added dresses and women's coats to their stock and by 1860 they had included underwear, millinery and shoes which were sold in separate departments. The Bouçicauts differed very greatly from contemporary traders in their subtle appreciation of *customer psychology*, thought by scoffing competitors to be "du romantisme en boutique", but in fact a major breakthrough which subsequent retailers exploited even further by enlisting the aid of designers and architects. This new appreciation of customer psychology manifested itself initially in three differing innovations. In the first of these the Bouçicauts daringly abolished the traditional practice of haggling over every item in the shop and instead offered only goods on which the prices were clearly marked. At the time this may have seemed like a take-it-or-leave-it gamble, but one can surmise that the shrewd Bouçicauts, aware of the fact that the social class of their customers was rising as they themselves prospered and could offer more sophisticated goods, assumed that whereas assistant cooks would cheerfully argue over the price of cabbages in local street markets, some 'gentlewomen' might find embarrassment in beating tradesmen up and down over the cost of every yard of *Valenciennes* they coveted for a gown.

Another innovation dear to the heart of modern consumers, was the establishment of the right of customers to exchange goods or to have their money refunded, but the third innovation of this enterprising husband and wife team is astonishing to late 20th-century shoppers who assume they can enter any shop or store at will. Unwitting adaptors of the Mae West adage that a man in the house is worth two on the street[4], the Bouçicauts drew more of spendthrift Paris into their net by granting the public *total freedom of access* to their establishment. Until that time, contemporary Parisian retailers regarded their shops as private places or extensions of their own homes, which they frequently in fact were, and those who entered such a shop were assumed to be doing so on purposeful business and were encouraged to be even more purposeful by a civil but stifling sense of obligation to buy. As keen amateur psychologists, the Bouçicauts realised that whereas one could make a moderate living from supplying a demand that was verbally expressed, one could make an infinitely more brilliant career by supplying a desire that the customer *did not know she had until she had entered the premises*. Thus, the Bouçicauts pioneered the idea of the department store as a building purposely designed for fashionable public assembly and which, by the use of display techniques and eye-catching design which developed rapidly over the next decades, supplanted the commercial principle of *supply* with that of *consumer seduction*.

A natural development of the seduction principle was to be found in yet another Bouçicaut innovation: the instigation of periodic sales of goods at bargain prices. Every shopper, then and now, loves a genuine bargain, but perhaps the most winning psychology of the 'sale' was the fact that by spreading out laces, ribbons, and fine haberdashery and fabrics of every kind in tangled heaps, informality of display was pressed to its furthest extreme and with it potential customers were given an unbridled tactile access to goods in the manner of infants romping with water. The Bouçicauts in fact pioneered what is now less elegantly known as the 'soft sell' where external pressure to buy is replaced by the prompting of individual libido freely operating in a highly informal sales situation. Although the late 20th-century British press still fills column inches with news of sales' 'battlefields' as regularly as January annually appears, it requires considerable imaginative effort to visualise the utterly devastating impact which pioneer sales had on the late 19th-century female public when social transactions of any kind were highly formalised and the external display of inner libidinousness was rigorously suppressed in polite society. Tactile access to goods during sales was in fact a literally riotous innovation, particularly since the bulk of goods were in ordinary circumstances, stored in quite elaborate showcases and banks of drawers, although the public was freely admitted to wander through the store and look. Some of the finest and most detailed photographs now extant of showcases *in situ* in a late 19th-century department store may be seen in Bedford Lemere's distinguished photographs, taken in 1895, of the lingerie and millinery departments at Charles Jenner & Company, Princes Street, Edinburgh, built by William Hamilton Beatie between 1893–95 (see pages 24–27).

The Bouçicauts completed their innovations by giving guarantees of quality on higher-priced goods and by instituting a daily delivery service to all parts of Paris. Business became so successful that they were soon able to dramatically undercut competitors in pricing by selling large quantities at a lower profit margin – a practice which completely reversed the contemporary retailing principle of a slow stock turn-over and a high mark-up. Once initiated and seen to be extraordinarily successful, their methods were soon copied in Paris and 1865 saw the opening of the first Le Printemps department store in that city, followed by the opening in new premises of the store, La Belle Jardinière, originally founded by Pierre Parissot, in 1866. As the 1870s arrived, the original Bon Marché itself was ready for expansion into new premises and in 1876 the new Magasin au Bon Marché, thought to be the first genuine department store of any significant size in Europe, was built in the rue de Sèvres by L. C. Boileau (1837–    ) and the great French engineer Gustave Eiffel (1832–1923).

Well-defined photographs of the interiors of such stores built in Paris during the 1870s and '80s – Le Printemps expanded into a new store built by Paul Sédille (1836–1900) on the corner of the rue de Rome and the Boulevard Haussmann between 1881–89 – are naturally difficult to discover, but for a brilliant picture in words of the hectic innovation in Parisian commercial life during this period we are fortunate to have in the novel *Bonheur des Dames* by Émile Édouard Zola (1840–1902) an unsurpassed eye-witness account.[5] With his sharp, inquisitive journalist's eye coupled to a belief in literary 'Naturalism' by which his characters, their actions and their physical environment are described in as close and

'accurate' detail as possible in the manner of a scientific enquiry, *Bonheur des Dames* is an overwhelming account of the rise of a fictional Parisian department store under its ruthless and sensual proprietor, Octave Mouret. Throughout the novel Mouret's commercial success is attributed to his unique ability to combine financial daring with *artistic* panache and the novel is full of detailed design information. Here, for example, is a description of one of Mouret's many design triumphs: a dazzling and breath-taking entirely white display which succeeds in making the besieging crowds of shoppers look "black, like December skaters on a lake in Poland":

"It was the stupendous sight of the great exhibition of household linen which was holding up the ladies. First of all, surrounding them, there was the entrance hall, with light windows, and paved with mosaics, in which displays of inexpensive goods were drawing the voracious crowd. Next there were galleries leading out, of a dazzling whiteness like a polar vista, a whole snowy region unfolding with the endlessness of steppes draped with ermine, a mass of glaciers lit up beneath the sun. The same whiteness as that in the outside windows was repeated there, but it was heightened and on a colossal scale, burning from one end of the enormous nave to the other with the white blaze of a conflagration at its height. There was nothing but white, all the white goods from every department, an orgy of white, a white star the steady radiance of which was blinding at first, and made it impossible to distinguish any details in the midst of this unparalleled whiteness. Soon the eyes grew accustomed to it: to the left of the Monsigny gallery there stretched out white promontories of linens and calicoes, white rocks of sheets, table-napkins and handkerchiefs; while in the Michodière gallery on the right, occupied by the haberdashery, hosiery and woollens, white edifices were displayed made of pearl buttons; there was a huge set-piece made of white socks, a whole hall covered with white swansdown and lit up from above by a shaft of light. But the main source of light was that radiated from the central gallery, where the ribbons and fichus, the gloves and silks were situated. The counters disappeared beneath the white of silks and ribbons, of gloves and fichus. Around the iron pillars froths of white muslin were twining up, knotted from place to place with white scarves. The staircases were decked with white draperies, draperies of piqué alternating with dimity, which ran all along the banisters, encircling the halls right up the second-floor; and the ascending whiteness was taking wing, thronging and disappearing like a flight of swans. From the domes the whiteness was falling back again in a rain of eiderdown, a sheet of huge flakes of snow: white blankets and white coverlets were waving in the air, hung up like banners in a church; long streams of pillow-lace were interlaced and seemingly suspended like swarms of white butterflies, humming there motionless; laces were quivering everywhere, floating like gossamer against a summer sky, filling the air with their white breath. And over the silk counter in the main hall there was a tent made of white curtains hanging down from the glass roof, which was the miracle, the altar of this cult of white. There were muslins, gauzes, guipures, flowing in frothy waves, while sumptuous embroidered tulles and lengths of oriental silk and silver lamé served as a background to this gigantic decoration, which smacked both of the tabernacle and of the bedroom. It looked like a great white bed, its virginal whiteness waiting, as in legends, for the white princess, for she who would one day come, all powerful, in her white bridal veil.

'Oh! It's fantastic!' the ladies were repeating. 'Extraordinary'!"[6]

Within a year of the Magasin au Bon Marché opening in its new premises it found an imitator both in name and organisation across the English Channel. This was the Bon Marché built at Brixton, London in 1877 by a local printer, Smith, who had won a fortune on a racehorse called Rosebery and decided to sink the greater part of it in opening his own new department store. Unfortunately, Mr 'Rosebery' Smith, as he was thereafter known, proved to be no Octave Mouret and although the store survives today as a member of the John Lewis Partnership, it was for its first proprietor a commercial disaster. Nor when first built was the Brixton Bon Marché particularly distinguished architecturally, but its significance lies in the fact that it is thought to be the first building in Britain to be commissioned by a company which regarded itself as a department store from the outset, as opposed to similar structures commissioned by long-established companies which had begun life as traditional grocers or drapers.[7]

Despite this over-optimistic attempt at Brixton, the fretful brilliance which characterised the new mode of shopping in Paris from the 1860s onwards does not seem to have made its glittering début in Britain until considerably later. Indeed, a glance at the Chronology of Shop Design on page 12 will show that in company with the major cities of the rest of Europe and of course excluding Paris, the massive rebuilding programmes of already established department stores in Britain did not begin until the 1890s. A contributor to *The Fortnightly Review*, writing in 1895, was at pains to remind her readers, dazzled perhaps by the current ascent of Harrods Ltd in Knightsbridge, London, that a mere 25 years before, English shops were distinguished only by their smallness and inferiority, the lack or feebleness of display in their windows, their concentration on one speciality only and above all, an unremittingly conservative manner of carrying on business.[8] In comparison with the fashionable gregariousness which the French had introduced into shopping, Lady Jeune's account of a visit to a traditional English draper during the 1870s makes formal and funereal reading:

"An afternoon's shopping was a solemn and dreary affair, when one was received at the door of the shop by a solemn gentleman in black, who in due time delivered one over to another solemn gentleman, and perhaps again to a third, who found one a chair, and in a sepulchral tone of voice uttered some magic words, such as, 'Silk, Mr Smith,' or 'Velvet, Mr A.' and then departed to seek another victim."[9]

Another innovation which this British *fin-de-siècle* shopper noted and which contributed a great deal to the success of the late 19th-century department store, was the employment of large numbers of female shop assistants. Apart from the economic abuse of female labour in this sphere which Zola forcefully noted, and which, as we well know, was not confined to late 19th-century entrepreneurs, the employment of women in shops concerned with the sale of fabrics, haberdashery and fashion accessories had a more honourable motive. During the latter decades of the 19th century the achievement of total ensemble in a fashionably dressed woman reached a new stage of complexity, beginning from the body outwards with a series of corset designs which were in themselves civil engineering feats worthy of Eiffel. Should proof be needed that the object of women's costume during this period was not only to enhance the wearer and define social position, but simply to baffle, this passage from 'The Heart of Life', serialised in *The Fortnightly Review* during the 1890s as a pale imitation of the great Ouida, indicates the subtle complexity of women's costume in these last decades before suffrage released them from luxurious imprisonment in the Western harem:

"Countess Shimna at first was not aware of his presence . . . and the simplicity of her attitude and expression was rendered doubly striking by contrast with her toilette, which, though its own way equally simple, betrayed in every detail the subtlety of Parisian art . . . Points in her dress for which, man-like, he had no name, subtle coquetteries of colour, and fit, and fold, filled him with thoughts of far-off continental dissipation, of the glitter of casinos, and of whisperings under lamp-lit foliage."[10]

Clearly, if Countess Shimna's distinguished admirer found her ensemble effective but bewildering, how much more so would those funereal drapers, particularly when requested to assist in its artistic compilation. Instead, quick, deft shop-girls, with an eye for rapidly changing fashion and an ability to advise on colours under artificial lighting, were employed to constructively assist female customers in these emphemerally complicated matters. This transition of shop assistants from dreary drapers to modish consultants in late 19th-century department stores may be reflected in the appearance of the slang-term 'shop-masher' *circa* 1885 meaning, according to Eric Partridge, "a very well, or much, dressed shop-assistant."[11]

But the attraction of society women to late 19th-century department stores depended not only on the sale of exquisite goods or deft and helpful service, but on presenting an image of such stores as *respectable* places of public assembly at which unaccompanied women could congregate without damage to their fragile reputations. Harrods Ltd of London had already established itself as an institution frequented by fashionable but highly *risqué* celebrities when, in 1885, its management decided to give limited credit to approved customers and the first list of those permitted credit included the names of Oscar Wilde, Ellen Terry and Lily Langtry.[12]

But although such personalities were a flattering addition to their clientele, most managements of late 19th-century department stores were at pains to attract more Caesars' wives of substantial income and less brilliant mavericks of precarious finances.[13] As, for example, at the great Wertheim department store built on Berlin's Leipzigerstrasse by Alfred Messel between 1896–99 (see page 38) this was done initially by commissioning buildings of imposing solidity of fabric, for the 19th-century seems to have regarded jerry-building as the outward and visible sign of a lack of moral probity not only in the builder but the occupier, and in common with the great majority of European public buildings of the period, a use of inflated Classically-derived detail also emphasised the links, both in riches and military power between Western 19th-century civilisation and that of the equally colonising Roman Empire (see page 39).

A building fabric that was all too visibly above suspicion was therefore one way in which the proprietors of department stores could make it plain that however commercially novel their establishments, they were not overheated dens of vice into which society women used, in polite theory at least, to a circuit of escorted visits to opera houses, race meetings and private *soirées*, need fear to trust themselves. Indeed, Gordon Selfridge, whose new department store was being built on London's Oxford Street by Daniel Burnham and R. Frank Atkinson in 1908, regarded himself as the very emperor of architecturally-minded store proprietors when he said, "Business is fine, columns are fine, why should not a business have columns?"[14] But not content with this solid, physical respectability, Selfridge pressed the idea further of the store as a 'safe', paternalistic and all-caring mansion able to provide every want and in which he as proprietor temporarily replaced husband, father or brother as the protective head of a social unit, by his introduction of the slogan, 'Why Not Spend The Day At Selfridges?'[15] Harrods too were already working on these all-caring lines when, after the installation of their first escalator in November 1898, two attendants were stationed at the top of it to revive alarmed customers with cognac and sal volatile.[16]

With such inflated moral and financial responsibilities as these, proprietors of department stores were finding it difficult to personally supervise the seductive display of their wares in the way Octave Mouret had done and specialisation in this design field is said to have been introduced to London by Gordon Selfridge who summoned Marshall Field's head window-dresser, Goldsman, from Chicago to supervise display at his Oxford Street store.[17] Similarly, by early

20th-century when department stores had become massive, rambling institutions a need was felt to somehow use design to pull the image of a store together and present it to the public as a well-defined commercial entity. Here again, Selfridge drew on the panache of already well-established American sales practice by the use of Selfridge Green as a house colour for the co-ordination of carpets, wrapping paper, bill-heads and delivery vans, a commonplace now, but then highly novel in London.[18]

Perhaps Gordon Selfridge succeeded in making his new store just a little too substantial in attempted architectural effect, for in its early days it did not attract *quite* the same clientele as Harrods and its design, although highly pleasing to its proprietor, surprised even that section of Edwardian society which looked on a fine figure of a building with the same spirited, moustache-twirling appreciation as it looked through conservatory palms at a fine figure of a woman. ''Don't you be so Selfridge,'' in fact became a catch-phrase among young Edwardian architectural wits like Sir Albert Richardson.[19]

But whatever one's opinion of the design of this massive Edwardian paen to commercialism in London, the 20th century dawned in Brussels on a series of shops designs of such astonishing elegance, stemming from total structural and decorative clarity, that they are incontrovertibly regarded today as ranking among the masterpieces of *fin-de-siècle* commercial building. These are the shops, both large and small, designed by the *Art Nouveau* master Baron Victor Horta (1861–1947).

Just as the Japanist Arthur Lazenby Liberty played a significant part in the English Aesthetic Movement by his dissemination of oriental fabric designs from his shop East India House, opened in Regent Street, London in 1875, the spread of *Art Nouveau* in Europe was initially closely associated with the opening of small shops, often in themselves *Art Nouveau* showcases, for the work of new craftsmen and artists. The very term *Art Nouveau* is said to have been initiated as the name of a shop built in the rue de Provence, Paris by L.-B Bonnier (1856–1946) for the Hamburg art dealer Samuel B.ng in 1895.[20] As a showcase for some of the best craftwork of the day, this was one of many small *avant-garde* shops which sprang up in Europe as disseminators of new design during the 1890s, including the Compagnie Japonais, Brussels which was showing English wallpaper and metalwork in 1891; Keller und Reiner of Berlin; the Uiterwyck craft shop in The Hague; Julius Meier-Graefe's La Maison Moderne opened in 1898[21] and the Hohenzollern Kunstgewerbehaus, Berlin built by Henri van de Velde (1865–1957) in 1899 (see page 44). Although Bing's shop, L'Art Nouveau is thought to be of comparatively little architectural interest, it set a fashion not only in its goods but in shop-fronts which spread rapidly to most Continental cities and even to England and America where *Art Nouveau* otherwise hardly penetrated.[22] Another important disseminator of *Art Nouveau* shop-fronts and fittings was the Belgian architect Paul Hankar (1859–1901)[23] whose façade for The English Modern Company, built at Brussels in 1897, is shown in page 43.

The most important single work of Victor Horta himself is generally thought to be his Maison du Peuple built in Brussels on a curiously shaped site for the Brussels branch of the Workers' Party between 1896–99 and demolished in 1967. The Maison du Peuple was conceived as something of a late 19th-century community centre and was a multi-use building with an auditorium at the top, in which Horta was able to catch a good deal of ''the volumetric lightness previously associated with temporary exhibition buildings only.''[24] The auditorium of the Maison du Peuple is very frequently illustrated, but the complex also contained a department store, the façade of which is shown in page 30 and a large café which seems in its interior design to be a gentle satire on the overweening holiness of the high altar in traditional church building (see page 31).

Of the myriad of *Art Nouveau* department stores which sprang up like metal flowers across Europe during this period, such as the poppy-canopied Magazzino Contratti built by Luigi Broggi (1851–1926)[25] at Milan in 1903; Horta's own Grand Bazar, Frankfurt of 1903; the Grand Bazar de la rue de Rennes built by H.-B. Gutton in Paris between 1902–03; and the celebrated Samaritaine department store again built at Paris by Franz Jourdain and Henri Sauvage in 1905,[26] Horta's major commercial building in Brussels, the department store A l'Innovation, emerges as the most elegant of the *Art Nouveau*, department-store genre, although it precedes the others in date. Built in the rue Neuve, Brussels in 1901 and most unhappily destroyed by fire in 1967 (a bad year for Horta in Brussels) the façade of A l'Innovation with its enormous areas of glazing, not only pointed forwards to a time when walls would be relieved of their load-bearing role to become light-conveying transparent envelopes, but is an example of *Art Nouveau* decorative design genuinely conceived on a fully architectural scale and without any sense of that strenuous inflation which can occur when a decorative mode, used principally for interior decoration, is made to take its place on the greater scale of a street.[27] The façade of A l'Innovation and decorative details of the interior are shown in pages 50–53.

Of the glazing of A l'Innovation, Victor Horta wrote in his unpublished *Memoires*,

''. . . It might be thought that this glazing, and the rake of the pillars supporting the galleries which were designed to broaden the glazed ceiling, were a mere whim of the architect! Far from it: these areas of glass answered the need to bring in daylight, otherwise called natural light, as widely as possible; to provide the conditions under which the public would wish to inspect the goods for sale, whose colours would essentially be falsified by electric lights.''

He continues, ''. . . to draw the passer-by in from outside and make a purchaser of him, and once 'caught' to make him notice the smallest item on display . . . the customer's will and his desire to see, have been the architect's main objectives. He has aimed above all to give an impression of wholeness . . . and has prescribed the only possible materials: iron and steel. These materials were not new but have seldom been used in an artistic shape because of the hostility the public has shown towards them.''[28]

The next and last major wave of department store building in Europe gained its impetus from Germany during the 1920s in a series of designs which seem, at first glance, to be a century away from those of Horta rather than some 25 years. These were the stores built by the highly influential German architect Erich Mendelsohn (1887–1953) beginning with that built for C. A. Herpich & Sons on the Leipzigerstrasse, Berlin in 1924; the Petersdorff store at Breslau and the Schocken store at Stuttgart built in 1926–27, followed by another Schocken store, built on a potentially awkward wedge-shaped site at Chemnitz in 1928.[29] The façades of all the Mendelsohn stores built during the late 1920s have in common the long bands of horizontal fenestration (see page 99) which add to the lightness and grandeur already associated with Horta's A l'Innovation, a new sense of sophisticated visual tension by which we now distinguish much design of the 1920s whatever its status. With this series of designs Mendelsohn breathed a new and pervasive life into the department store as a building type and between 1927–35 there were in Europe few new department store projects with any pretension to progressiveness in design which did not fall directly under his influence.

In London the mantle of Mendelsohn fell gracefully and appropriately in Sloane Square, where the new Peter Jones department store was built between 1933–36 by J. Alan Slater, Arthur Hamilton Moberly and William Crabtree in conjunction with Sir Charles Reilly. In an article by Sir Charles Reilly published in *The Architectural Review* in 1935 when his contribution to the new Peter Jones store was already well advanced, Reilly not only took the opportunity of castigating the earlier design of most other celebrated department stores in London with his suggestion that columns properly belonged to the drapery business rather than to architecture, but totally rejected, or more probably failed to recognise, the importance of visually catering for architecturally extraneous consumerist fantasy in all shop building. With the admirable rationality of his period he felt instead that a department store should, on Mendelsohnian lines, develop distinct design characteristics of its own to the point at which it would be quite unnecessary for such a building type to pose either as a royal palace or an opulent commercial hotel. Unwittingly a forerunner of today's runners-up of hyper- and super-markets he felt in fact that a store was really nothing more than floor after floor of unimpeded selling space as large as the site and the by-laws would allow and in which "continuous layers of glass window" would alternate with "continuous layers of solid, just deep enough to satisfy the by-laws and cover the edges of the floors and the women's ankles . . ."[30] Returning to his Selfridge-style *bête noire* he added, "Surely it is a little ridiculous, if not embarrassing, to imagine some filmy little scrap of lingerie, or a pair of silk stockings, being sold behind Mr Selfridge's great imperial Columns?"[31] – nowadays an astonishing remark, particularly to young customers at the Biba department store in Kensington High Street, London, happily buying prune-coloured tights to the accompaniment of lavish, half-lighted pastiche and quadrophonically amplified nostalgic ditties. Proof that the new generation of consumers tacitly finds the Modern Movement approach to department-store building emotionally unsatisfactory must be shown here, where Biba's proprietors have assumed that their young customers prefer not the comfort and convenience of rationally organised sales areas, but an opulent and luxurious *shopping experience* lavishly based on an Art Deco pastiche which owes more to Oliver Bernard's Strand Palace Hotel, London built in 1929 (see page 104) than to any 20th-century department-store proto-type. Furthermore, the current thirst for an irrational shopping experience has reached such a rabid stage among youthful consumers, that in the short course of the 1970s alone, many proprietors of *chic* boutiques and cafés have been obliged to revise their décor almost annually, first rejecting *Art Nouveau* pastiche in favour of *Art Deco* and now disposing of that in favour of '40s Austerity or '50s Rock Americana, whilst keeping a weather eye on the imminent '60s Mod Revival.

Pandering to consumer fantasy rather than endeavouring to supply customer convenience did, of course, also go on in the design of small and exclusive shops which were constantly ripped out and yet again ephemerally refitted during the 1920s when leading architects were intent on transforming the look of the department store from that of the presidential apartments of the People's Republic of Vulgaria to physically comfortable, spacious and well-lighted sales areas. In the light of this, that ubiquitous decorative style of the 1920s and '30s known as Art Deco or Jazz Modern, which incorporated from year to year a variety of influences from the colouring of Diaghilev's Ballets Russes via Tutankhamenism and Aztec forms to Afro art, may be seen as the popular and decoratively eclectic response to the stripped and fervid rationalism that was going on upstairs in the drawing office. As the enthusiastic response in the mid-1970s to Julian Barnard's *The Decorative Tradition* has shown[32], despite the fact that architecture is an art principally concerned with the organisation of space, the public has always persisted in seeing it as an art concerned with the arrangement of *physical* elements and what is more elements which it would prefer to see imbued with figurative meaning. This preference has always been catered for in shop design, although with varying degrees of elegance and success, from the depiction of stylised cigar smoke on the walls of the Habana Company cigar shop built in Berlin by Henri van de Velde in 1898 (see page 40) to the coarsely luxurious D'Orsay perfume shop, fitted out in the rue de la Paix, Paris by the exclusive French design partnership of the 1920s, Süe et Mare. Here the strong pink ceiling was powdered with small gilded flowers in deference to the sweet-smelling products sold in the shop (see page 87), a literal approach to luxuriousness paralleled in contemporary Germany at the Bechstein pianoforte showrooms, Berlin, where Oskar Kaufmann drew on the tradition of German figurative wood carving in his decoration of the staircase with oblique wooden bands depicting Orpheus charming the wild beasts with his lyre (see page 93). Such designs as these recall the reaction of Berthold Brecht on his arrival at Berlin in 1920, "What tastelessness. But on what a level!"

Shops are in business to give the public what, at a price, it wants and both the importance and fascination of shop design lies in the fact that it was, and to some degree still is, one of the few kinds of public building in which accommodating designers are generally commissioned not to lead public taste too far ahead of its day, but to closely consider and follow it. The *taste* of building users is, as we know, quite a different thing from their *needs* and the following collection of photographs shows the confident taste of half a century displayed in all its splendid variety – both marvellously 'good' and riotously 'bad', but very rarely in that neutral limbo of white-painted hesitancy which not only characterises our present confusion but the tender and melancholy cynicism with which we regard the stylistic confidence of the past.

Gigantic façade and two interiors of the huge, glass-roofed covered market, Torgovye Ryadi, Red Square, Moscow, built by Alexander Nikanorovitch Pomerantsev between 1888–93 and now inhabited by Gosudarstvenny Universalny Magasin (GUM), the State Department Store

15

Left: furniture warehouse at Heelas of Reading *circa* 1892

Right: two views of the tea-rooms at Charles Jenner & Company, Princes Street, Edinburgh built by William Hamilton Beatie between 1893–95. In this piece of astonishing eclecticism a Jacobethan ceiling is unselfconsciously merged with miniature Ionic columns and Alhambra-style 'Moorish' piercing.

These and subsequent photographs of this store were taken by the distinguished Victorian photographer, Bedford Lemere, in 1895 and form one of the few, well-defined and extensive records of the interior of a late 19th-century department store now extant

Top left: ground-floor view of the glove and lace counters at Charles Jenner & Company

Left: overview of the haberdashery department at Charles Jenner & Company, taken from a first-floor gallery. The counter in the right foreground of the photograph displays a mass of artificial flowers, ostrich feathers and trimmings; beyond it lies the glove counter and on the left the entire counter is devoted to lace. Both over the counters and high overhead, the china lampshades hang like crisp lace handkerchiefs

Top right: fabrics hall of Charles Jenner & Company. The legends above the left-hand counter read from left to right: 'Prints,' 'Muslins,' 'Calicoes,' and 'Napery' and the chairs, both here and elsewhere in the building, have the store monogram 'C J' worked into their back rails

Right: continuation of the fabrics department at Charles Jenner & Company. The legends inscribed over the counters to the right read 'Plushes' and 'Silks'

Fancy goods department at Charles Jenner & Company showing a profusion of oriental lacquered work

**Right: gallery of china and glass at Charles Jenner & Company where the display technique is based on the principle that more is more**

**Above: two furniture galleries at Charles Jenner & Company**

22

24

The impression of an exotic aviary is achieved in this mingled display of fanciful hats and potted plants at Charles Jenner & Company

Lingerie display adjacent to the millinery department of Charles Jenner & Company. The bodices displayed at floor level have quite likely been artificially positioned there to aid the composition of the photograph

Bottom left, above and top right: continuation of a walk through the women's fashion department at Charles Jenner & Company, via evening mantles to children's and babies' wear

Centre right: view across the central well of Charles Jenner & Company. Appropriately, for a Princes Street store, the gallery railing incorporates thistle motifs

Bottom right: behind the scenes at Charles Jenner & Company's Moorish tea-rooms, showing some carefully staged plates of food

Far left: entrance of the department store in the Maison du Peuple complex, Brussels, built by Baron Victor Horta between 1896–99

Left and above: two interiors of the café at the Maison du Peuple

Left: bedding gallery at Heal & Son Limited, Tottenham Court Road, London, photographed by Bedford Lemere in 1896. This picture subsequently appeared in the catalogue of the Paris Exhibition of 1900

Above: two single brass beds draped as one in the bedding showrooms of Heal & Son Limited in 1896

Luxuriously draped corner bed in a
furniture showroom at Heal & Son
Limited in 1896

Above: display of furnishing fabrics and decorative draping techniques in the upholstery gallery at Heal & Son Limited in 1896. Suspended at cornice level is an array of roller and Venetian blinds

Top right: row of portly chairs in the upholstery gallery at Heal & Son Limited

Bottom left and right: two furniture showrooms at Heal & Son Limited in 1896

Left: view of the fabric counters in the Wertheim department store, Leipzigerstrasse, Berlin built by Alfred Messel between 1896–99

Above: decadent Roman anta, decorated with peacocks and pierced by a dwarf colonnade, supporting a huge coffered arch at the Wertheim department store, Berlin

Elegant interior of the Habana Company cigar shop, Berlin, designed by Henri van de Velde in 1898, with stylised painted decoration representing cigar smoke

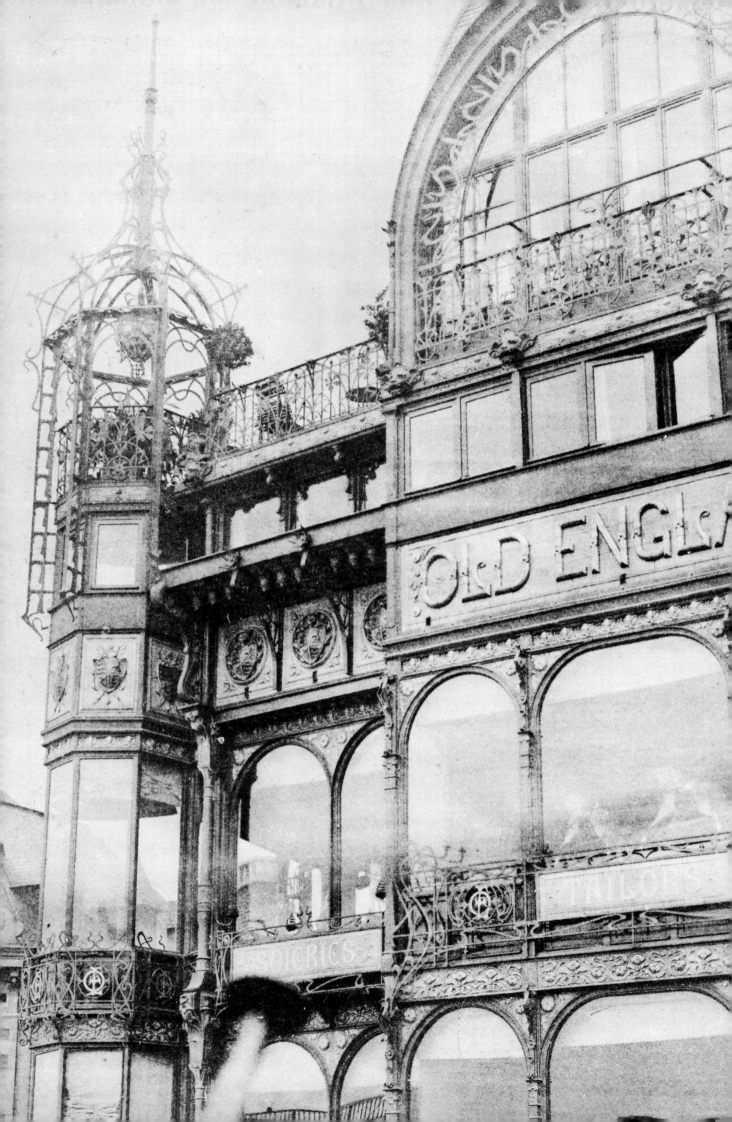

HYGIENE · MEUBLES · ANGLAIS · CONFORT

Bedroom-suites    THE ENGLISH MODERN COMPANY    Bedsteads

Above: façade of The English Modern Company, Brussels, designed by the disseminator of *Art Nouveau* shop-fronts and fittings, Paul Hankar, in 1897

Far left and left: two details of the façade of the Old England department store, rue Montagne de la Cour, Brussels built by Paul Saintenoy in 1899. As part of the English theme, a lift conveyed shoppers to a 'Tea Terrace' at the top of the store, from which a panoramic view of Brussels might be enjoyed. Another branch was built in the rue Rampe de Flandre, Ostend

# KUNST IM HANDWERK

# AUSSTELLUNG UND VERKAUF

Königl. Preussischer
K.u.K. Oesterreichischer
Grosshzgl. Badischer Hoflieferant.

## Hohenzollern K

13

Behting

FABRIK

HOHENZOLLERN
KUNSTGEWERBEHAUS

Kleinstrasse
Kymann

LEIPZIGERSTRASSE

GEÖFFNET:
Wochentags 9-7 Uhr
Sonntags (Wintermonate) 12-3 Uhr

Dauerkarten zu 3 M.
Tageskarten zu 1 M.

Left: façade of the Hohenzollern Kunst-gewerbehaus, Leipzigerstrasse, Berlin, built by Henri van de Velde in 1899: one of many sophisticated *fin-de-siècle* craft shops which disseminated the work of *Art Nouveau* designers throughout Europe

Above: oval decorative panel from a poultry and game department of a shop in the English grocery chain of J. Sainsbury Limited, executed *circa* 1900. Decoration was felt to be an important factor in attracting customers to Sainsbury shops

Interior of a small general store in Berlin photographed *circa* 1900. Some 30 years later, a shop of this traditional character represented a nostalgic ideal to the Nazi Party which denounced sophisticated department stores and their customers as decadent and 'un-German'. This hostility culminated in the 'Kristallnacht' of 1938 during which 29 Jewish-owned department stores were burned

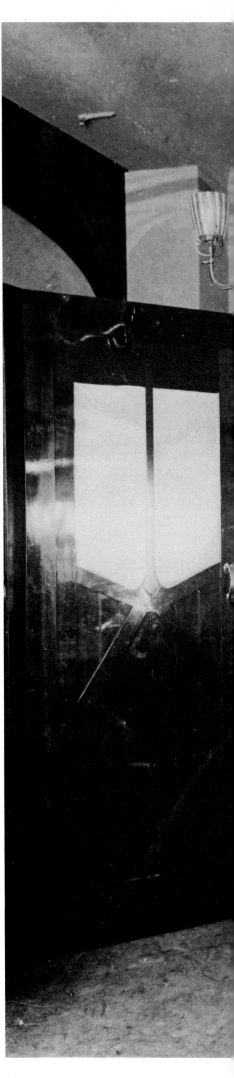

Right: interior of the Haby barber's shop, Berlin, designed by Henri van de Velde for Haby the Prussian Imperial Barber in 1900

Above: retail department of the Hygienic Dairies, Blackheath, London photographed *circa* 1900. The floor is made of black and white marble squares and the walls are covered with Minton's majolica in cream with a dado of sage green

Top: butter dairy of the Hygienic Dairies, Blackheath, reached from the retail department by two marble steps. The proprietors prided themselves that the butter-making process was fully exposed to public view and that the butter was never touched by human hand. The large churn on the left of the photograph was known as the 'Victoria'

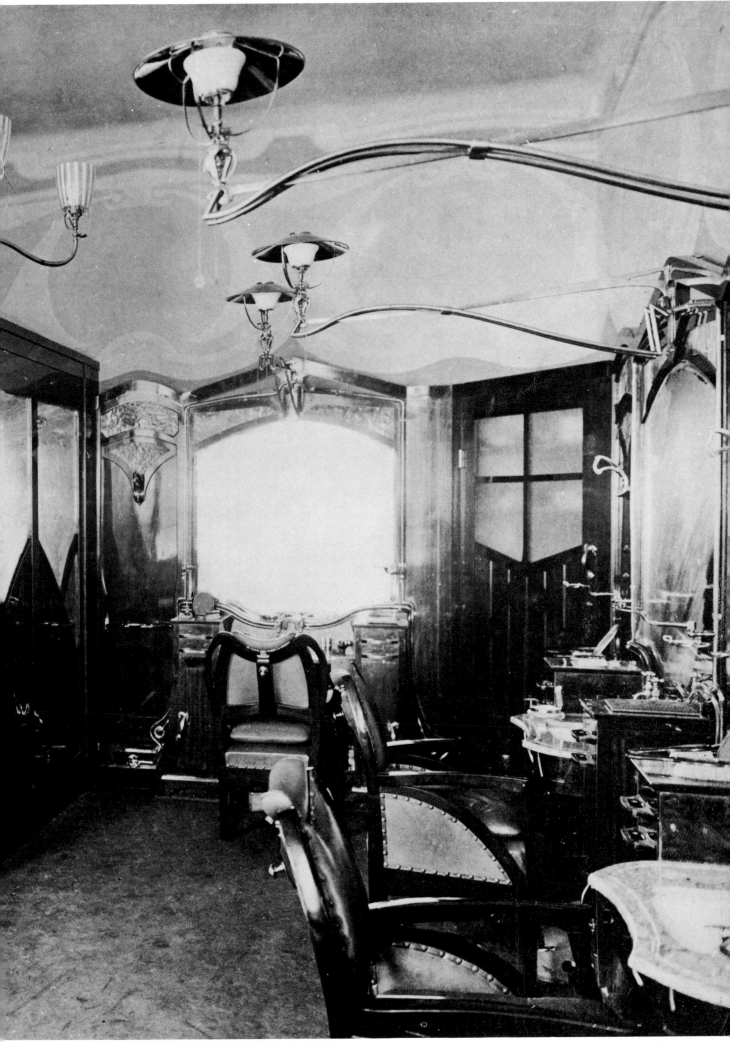

Left: extensively glazed façade of the department store A l'Innovation, rue Neuve, Brussels, built by Baron Victor Horta in 1901

Far left: glass cupola over the central patio of A l'Innovation

Above: detail of the recessed floors and sinuous light fittings of the central patio of A l'Innovation

51

'Whiplash' metalwork in the gallery railing of
A l'Innovation, Brussels

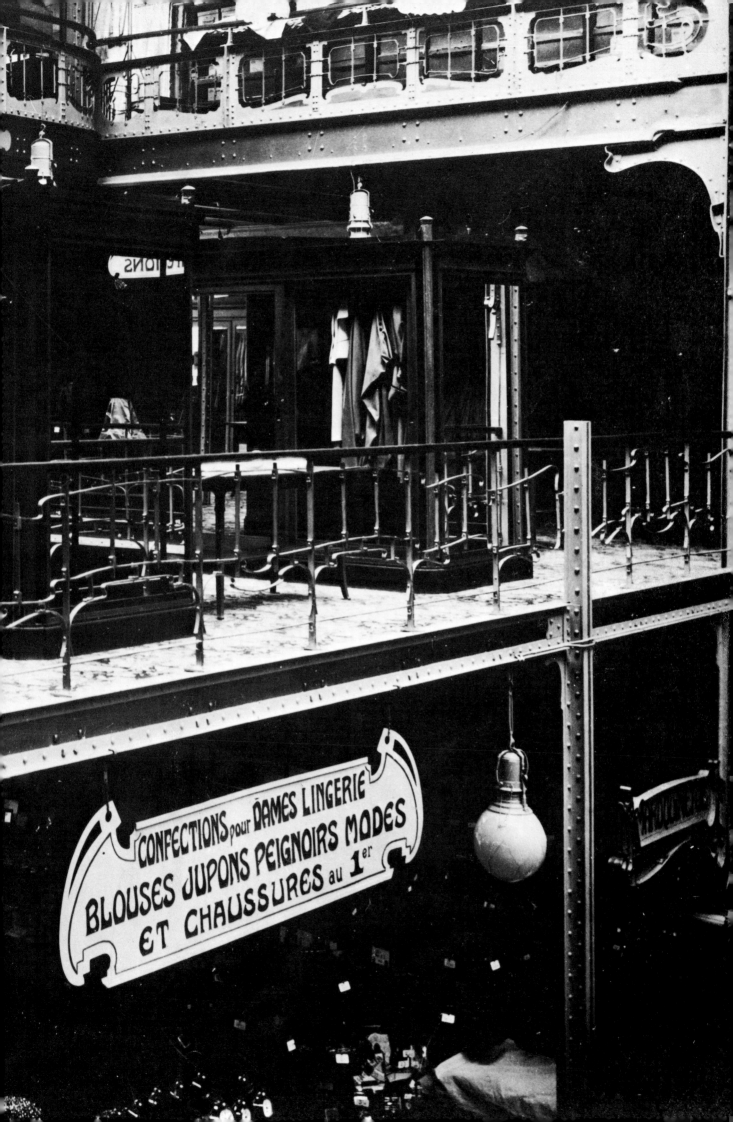

Left: poultry display in the Meat Hall at Harrods Limited which, as the showpiece of the store, was decorated by the great, late 19th-century British ceramicist W. J. Neatby

Above: section of the series of twenty ceramic medallions illustrating rural scenes with animals and hunters executed in 1902 by W. J. Neatby

Top: detail of a ceramic medallion showing a boar

Bakery department at Harrods Limited, Knightbridge, London, built by Stevens and Hunt between 1901–05

Far right: showroom of the Wolfers Jewellery Store, rue d'Arenberg, Brussels built by Baron Victor Horta in 1906

Above: interior of the Kärnter Bar, Kärnter Durchgang, Vienna designed by Adolf Loos in 1907 and in which a skilful use of mirrors disguises very small dimensions

Right: ceramic representation of King Edward VII and Prince George travelling in a Sedança de Ville: the centrepiece of a continuous tiled frieze by Gilardoni et Fils of Paris in the entrance hall of the Michelin car showrooms, Fulham Road, London, built by François Espinasse in 1909

Interior of a tobacconist's shop in Copenhagen, photographed *circa* 1906

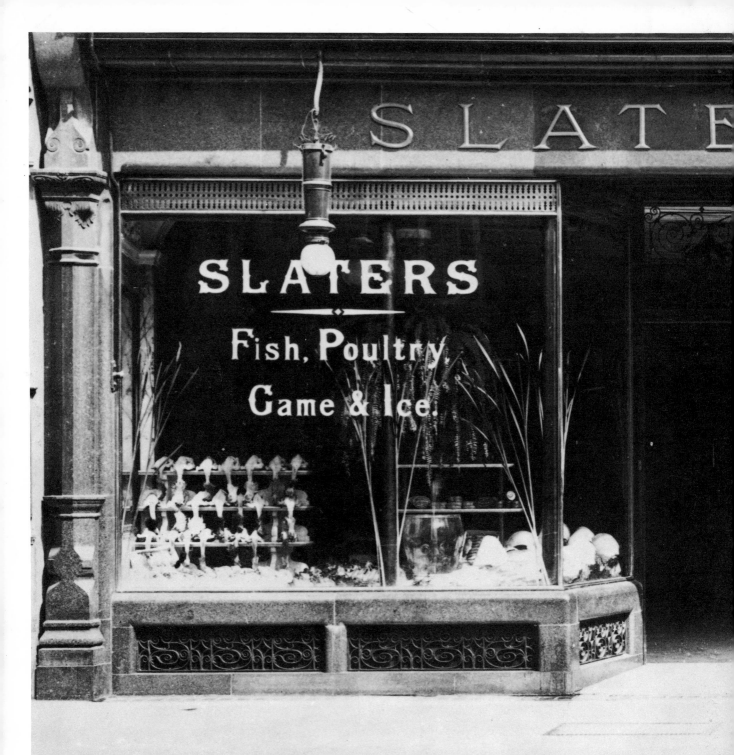

Entrance and interiors of the 'high-class provisioners' Slater & Company, Kensington High Street, London, photographed shortly before opening day in July 1909

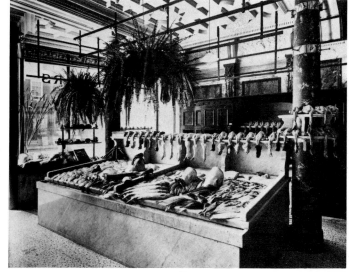

Right: interior of the Goldmann & Salatsch outfitters' shop, Michaelerplatz, Vienna, designed by Adolf Loos in 1910

Above: view of the upper sales floors and the glass roof with coloured banding at the Tietz department store, Berlin photographed in 1910

Far right: carpet department of the Tietz department store, photographed *circa* 1910, showing a display of children's clothes and baby carriages on the first-floor gallery above

View of the central hall of the Tietz department store, Alexanderplatz, Berlin taken from a first-floor gallery in 1910

Interior of The English Shop, in which umbrellas and walking sticks naturally figure prominently, built in the rue Marché aux Herbes, Brussels by Paul Hamesse *circa* 1910. This was one of a series of export shops which formed direct outlets for English luxury goods as far east as Moscow

MANICURE
2/6

Eau de Lilac
FRICTION

Eau de Lave
FRICTION

CHIROPODY

Eau de Quinine
FRICTION

Hairdressing saloon at the Hotel Cecil, London photographed
by Bedford Lemere in January 1911

Details of the Café Jama Michalikowa or 'Michael's Pit', Cracow, decorated in 1911 from designs by Karol Frycz for the literary cabaret *Zielony Balonik* or 'The Queer Little Balloon'. Frycz (1874–1963) was a theatrical designer and producer and one of the leading *Art Nouveau* decorators in Poland

Far left: doorway with turned wooden pillars surmounted by a mirror-tiled cartouche

Bottom left: interior of the Café Jama Michalikowa showing the traditional Polish *Szopka* or Nativity puppet theatre with which customers were entertained at Christmas-time

Left: upholstered double settle showing an owl in flight

Above: pipe smoke represented in coloured glass on the façade of the Vinche pipe works and shop, rue Marché aux Herbes, Brussels, designed by Paul Hamesse during the 1920s

Right: façade of the Phryne lingerie and accessories shop, built in the rue du Pont Neuf, Paris, during the 1920s, with a typical Art Deco sun-ray burst over the doorway

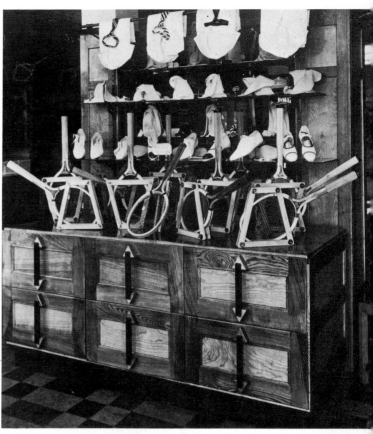

Left: interior of the first Harker's Sports Shop, Brussels designed by Lucien François in 1921

Top: *sportif* wooden storage boxes in the first Harker's Sports Shop

Above: jewellery department of the Grand Magasin de la Bourse, Brussels, opened in 1872 and photographed here *circa* 1920

Far right: staircase and reception desk of the Girault hairdressing shop, Boulevard des Capucines, Paris, by the fashionable Art Deco interior designers Azéma, Edrei et Hardy in 1923

Centre right: staircase detail in the department store De Bijenkorf or 'the beehive' built by P. L. Kramer in Grotemarkstraat, The Hague between 1924–26

Right: jagged galleries running round the central well of De Bijenkorf, The Hague

Top: detail of the basement staircase at the department store C. A. Herpich & Sons, Leipzigerstrasse, Berlin built by Erich Mendelsohn in 1924

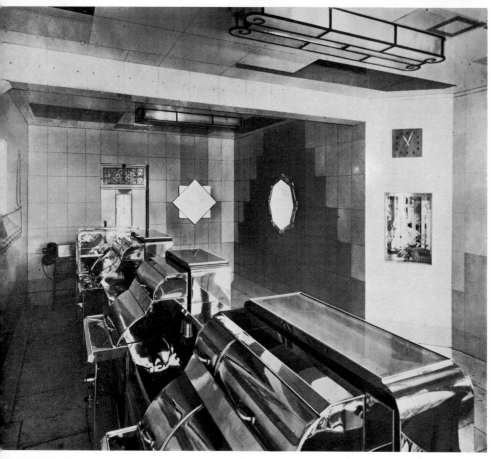

Above: two interiors of The Silver Grid fish and chip shop, Sunderland shortly before opening day in 1925. The *penchant* of Art Deco designers for chrome coincided so readily with the need for large, hygienic expanses of shiny metal in fish-frying equipment that 'Frying-Tonight Deco' has been the traditional mode for the British fish and chip shop ever since

Right: interior of the Rody-Bar, rue Lafayette, Paris designed during the early 1920s by J. & J. Martel

Left: peculiar tea-room in Berlin with yellow lacquered furniture, blue upholstery and orange light fittings designed by Ernst Friedmann during the mid-1920s

Above: counter with a circular inset display case in a '20s tea-shop in Copenhagen designed by Helweg-Møller

Below: Parisian-Pompeian interior of the Gabilla perfume shop, rue Faubourg St Honoré, Paris. The purpose-woven carpet suggests marble, the hanging lamp is made of bronze and alabaster and the tripod table is of green bronze. Although it has not been possible to date this and examples on pages 83–93 with total accuracy, they were all designed between 1920–28 and have been included to show the wayward and sometimes *chic* eclecticism which, despite the brilliant example of the German architectural *avant-garde*, pervaded the design of smaller shops during this period. In such projects, clients did not want architecture but decoration

Right: decorative details from the façade of the Colette et Suzy lingerie shop, opened in Paris *circa* 1925

Far right: Oriza-Legrand perfume shop in the Grands Boulevards, Paris fitted out in the Louis XVI manner with powder blue as the dominant colouring and panels of painted decoration

Bottom right: D'Orsay perfume shop, rue de la Paix, Paris designed in 1926 by the French design partnership Süe et Mare who founded the influential Compagnie des Arts Français in 1919. Here, the furniture is made of African ebony; the marble walls are dove grey and the strong pink ceiling is powdered with gilded flowers in deference to the sweet-smelling products sold in the shop

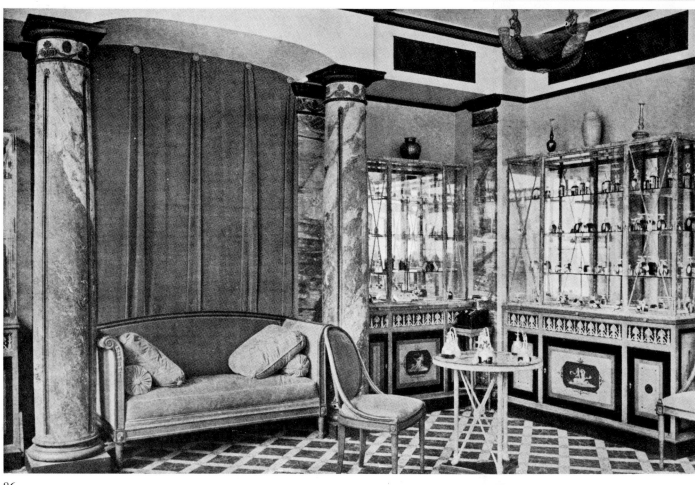

Above: Soutif Jewellery Shop, Avenue Victor Hugo, Paris designed by J. Landau

Top: marble washbasin in the ladies' section of the Figaro hairdressing salon, Berlin designed by Erich Teschemacher: a shop name calculated to ensnare Berlin's sophisticated opera-going public

Right: interior of the Pinoco handbag and trinket shop, Arcades des Champs-Élysées, Paris designed by the fashionable interior decorator of the 1920s, Deschanel

Left: extensive use of mirrors in the Pinet
shoe shop, Arcades des Champs-Élysées,
Paris designed by Süe et Mare *circa* 1925

Above: neo-Rococo sales floor of the
Olivier confectionery shop, Dresden designed by Karl Bertsch, Niemeyer and
the Deutsche Werkstätten

Right: dramatic bronze staircase at the
Cords textile shop, Berlin, designed by
Adolf Wollenberg

Right: Electrolux showrooms, Cologne, designed by Peter Baumann

Above: interior of the dress shop, Carron Soeurs, Boulevard Haussmann, Paris designed by René Herbst

Bottom right: Claridge's Shop in the Arcades des Champs-Élysées, Paris designed by Francis Jourdain

Top right: reception area of the Alfa-Romeo showrooms, rue Marbeuf, Paris designed by the cubist architect Robert Mallet-Stevens

Centre right: staircase with carved wooden bands, depicting Orpheus charming the wild beasts with his lyre, at the pianoforte showrooms of C. Bechstein, Berlin designed by Oskar Kaufmann

The celebrated Red Lacquer Room, Austin Reed Limited, Regent Street, London designed for the sale of travel and flying wear by P. J. Westwood and Emberton in 1925. All woodwork was finished in red lacquer inlaid with small 'real antique' panels and the freize, which consisted of a series of oil paintings depicting scenes and incidents during a voyage round the world, was painted by Fred Taylor RI who also designed the oriental cloisonné window

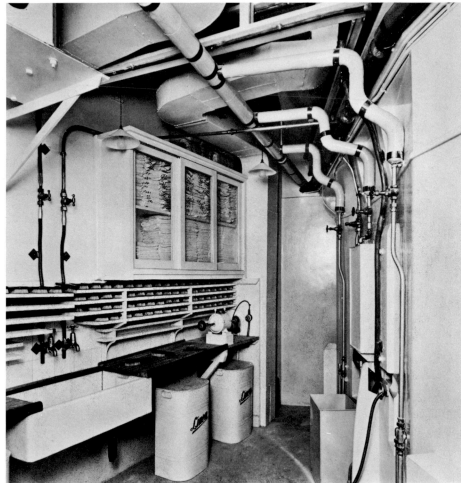

Top: the French Room, Austin Reed Limited, Regent Street, London designed for the sale of handmade shirts and night attire by P. J. Westwood and Emberton in 1925. Perhaps the choice of a late 18th-century French theme for a room selling these more intimate male garments suggests that the consumer fantasy operating here was *droit de seigneur*

Left: the Barber's Shop, Austin Reed Limited, designed with a wavy light fitting by P. J. Westwood and Emberton in 1925. The light fitting is still extant

Above: behind the scenes in the brush sterilising unit of the Austin Reed Barber's Shop

Far right: Petersdorff department store, Breslau (now Wroclaw) built by Erich Mendelsohn in 1927

Right: corner tower of the widely influential Schocken department store, Stuttgart, built by Erich Mendelsohn in 1926

Below: Burtol dry cleaning shop, Piccadilly, London designed by Chabot *circa* 1928

Restaurant with De Stijl tablecloths at the department store De Bijenkorf, Rotterdam, built by William Marinus Dudok between 1929–30

Right: food department at De Bijenkorf, Rotterdam

Far right: night view of The Times Furnishing Company, Birmingham designed by Cecil J. Eprile in 1929

Above: cool interior of the Crysede silk shop, Cambridge built by Wells Coates in 1929

Jazz Modern branch of the men's outfitter Dunn & Company
in the foyer of the Strand Palace Hotel, London built by
Oliver Bernard in 1929

Left: exterior of a genteel English café, Sisson's of Southport, built during the early 1930s by Arnold Ashworth & Sons

Above: interior view of a cake display in the window of a confectioner's shop in the Herrengasse, Vienna during the early 1930s

ECONOMICAL
RE FISH

FINEST
SCOTCH
KIPPERS
Per 10 ᴰ ᵗᵇ

SELEC
LONDON
DRIE
HADDO
Per 1 ᵗᴴᴸ

The Fish
displayed
to-day
comes from
ABERDEEN
HULL, GRIMSBY
MILFORD HAVEN
FLEETWOOD
NORTH SHIELDS

Spectacular fish display in the Food Hall of Harrods Limited,
Knightsbridge, London in February 1930

**Examples of display *bravura* at Harrods Limited during the 1930s including an exhibit with Britannia in Harrods' Home Farm-Produce Exhibition held between May 19th–24th, 1930**

Above: interior of the second Harker's Sports Shop, Brussels, showing a louvred glass balcony, designed by Lucien François in 1930

Left: cashier's desk in the second Harker's Sports Shop

Far left: view of the Man's Shop in Harrods Limited, Knightsbridge, London in October 1930

Right: gilt-bronze entrance door to Yardley's scent shop, Old Bond Street, London, designed by Reco Capey in 1931

Far right: unashamed Jacobethan pastiche in the Men's Hairdressing Lounge, Harrods Limited, Knightsbridge, London in 1931

Bottom right: Art Deco lift gates at Austin Reed Limited, Regent Street, London, designed by P. J. Westwood and Emberton *circa* 1925 and executed by Morris-Singer

Bottom centre: refrigerator display at Harrods Limited in 1932

Below: energetic use of glass and metal in the elevator shaft of the Grunfeld department store, Berlin built by Otto Firle in 1930

Left: airy seaside mural in a café at the Midland Hotel, Morecambe built by Oliver Hill in 1934

Above: view of the traditional galleried layout of Heal & Son Limited, Tottenham Court Road, London shortly before rebuilding in 1934

Top: display of bedroom furniture and fittings in the ground-floor showroom of Heal & Son Limited *circa* 1935

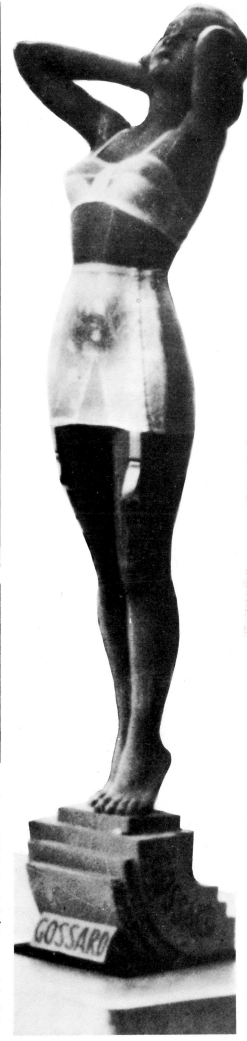

Left: new circular staircase at Heal & Son
Limited built by A. Dunbar Smith and
W. Cecil Brewer in 1934

Top: Black Cat, a statue bought during
the 1920s from L'Atelier Primavera, the
well-known department of decorative art
established at Les Grands Magasins du
Printemps, Paris in 1912. Originally
bought for display, it was subsequently
mounted on a permanent base by Sir
Ambrose Heal as a permanent feature of
a window alcove in the new circular staircase shown opposite

Right and above: the Strength-
Through-Joy Lady and The Gentlemanly
Bear, two familiar personalities to female
shoppers in search of corsetry and silk
stockings during the late 1930s

Three views of the Tailoring Room at Austin Reed Limited, Regent Street, London *circa* 1935, showing curved seating, storage and lighting combined in pillar units

Far left: floodlit exterior of Simpson's of Piccadilly, London built by Joseph Emberton in 1935

Left: walnut-veneered elevator interior with geometrical floor patterning reflecting the shape of the light fitting overhead at Simpson's of Piccadilly

Top: curving counter layout at Simpson's of Piccadilly

Above: reception area of the new Ladies' Hairdressing Department at Harrods Limited Knightsbridge, London in 1936

Right and centre: two interiors of cubicles in the new Ladies' Hairdressing Department at Harrods Limited

Far right: interior of the Dolores hat shop, Beak Street, London designed by Oliver Hill in 1937

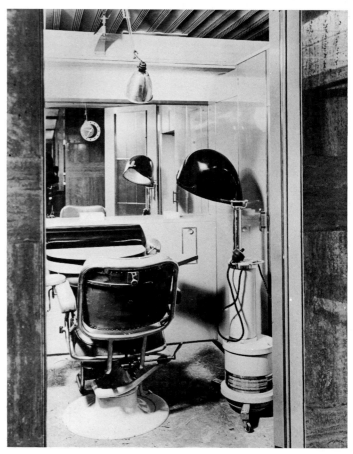

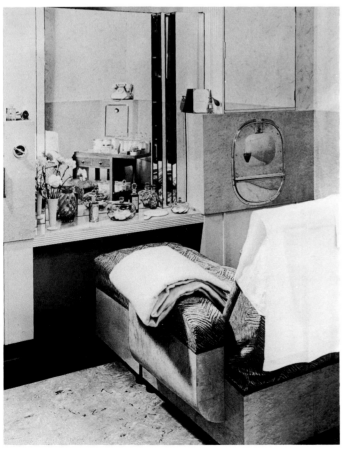

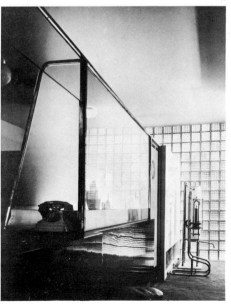

Far left: musical curtains in the His Master's Voice record showrooms, Oxford Street, London, designed by Joseph Emberton in 1938

Left: office counter showing a glass-brick wall for use as a display background at the Central London Electricity showrooms, Regent Street, London designed by E. Maxwell Fry in 1938

Above: staircase leading from the ground-floor showrooms of Central London Electricity Limited

# BIBLIOGRAPHY

**Adburgham, Alison** *Liberty's: a Biography of a Shop* London 1975

**Adburgham, Alison** *Shops and Shopping 1800–1914. Where, and in What Manner the Well-Dressed Englishwoman Bought Her Clothes* London 1964
An indispensable social history of shopping in Britain with some useful sidelights on developments in Europe

**Barnard, Julian** 'Some Work by W. J. Neatby' *The Connoisseur* November 1970, pages 165–71

**Barnard, Julian** 'Victorian on the Tiles': the Work of W. J. Neatby' *The Architect* September 1971, pages 46–51

**Barnard, Julian** 'The Master of Harrods' Meat Hall: W. J. Neatby' *Apollo* March 1970, pages 232–34
Three articles on the great Victorian ceramicist, whose designs still make the Meat Hall the showpiece of Harrods Ltd., Knightsbridge, London

**Braddell, Darcy** 'Little Shops of Paris' *The Architectural Review* July 1926, pages 4–9
Light period account of half-a-dozen perfume and lingerie shops built in Paris during the 1920s, including some work by Süe et Mare

**Boumphrey, Geoffrey** 'The Designers I: Sir Ambrose Heal' *The Architectural Review* July 1935, pages 39–40
Illustrates 'steady organic growth' in the design of furniture sold at Heal & Son Ltd., Tottenham Court Road, London

**Cantacuzino, Sherban** *A monograph on Wells Coates*, whose work included distinguished shop designs during the late '20s and early '30s, will be published by the Gordon Frazer Gallery Ltd., London in 1976

*Casabella* November 1959, No. 233: A special issue devoted to the work of Adolf Loos which illustrates, besides domestic work, the interiors of Goldmann & Salatsch, the Knižé tailor's shop and the Kärntner Bar

**Casteels, M.** *Henri van de Velde* Brussels 1932

**Davis, Dorothy** *A History of Shopping* London 1966

**de Maeyer, Charles** *Paul Hankar* Brussels 1962. Monograph on the controversial disseminator of *Art Nouveau* shop-fronts and fittings

**Dussell, K. K.** 'Drei Kaufhauser Schocken in Nürnberg, Stuttgart und Chemnitz von Erich Mendelsohn' *Modern Bauformen* November 1930, pages 461–84

*Edilizia Moderna* 8, 1899: plate 44 of this publication illustrates the Magazzini Boccioni, Rome; *Edilizia Moderna* 12, 1903: plate 26 illustrates Luigi Broggi's Magazzino Contratti, Milan

**Edwards, A. Trystan** *The Architecture of Shops* London 1933

'A Frieze Decoration at the Army & Navy Stores, London *The Architectural Review* July 1926, pages 10–15
Gives large full-colour illustrations of the A & N frieze by Gerald Moira, showing the peculiar eclecticism of decorative painting in the 1920s and the authentic coloration of the period

**Giedion, Siegfried** *Bauen in Frankreich: Eisen, Eisenbeton* Leipzig 1928
An important book which gives good illustrations of the Bon Marché, Paris

**Herbst, René** *Modern French Shop-Fronts and Their Interiors* John Tiranti & Company, London 1927
Contains excellent gravure plates showing a wide variety of the best 'smartistic' French work of the 1920s

**Hobhouse, Hermione** *A History of Regent Street* London 1975
A detailed and lavishly illustrated history of London's premier shopping street

**Holmdahl, Gustav et al** *Gunnar Asplund: Architect 1885–1940* Stockholm 1950
Contains photographs and plans of the Bredenberg store, Stockholm built between 1933–35

**Kiesler, Frederick** *Contemporary Art Applied to the Store and its Display* London 1930

**Kitson, Sydney** 'Liberty's, Argyll Place, London' *The Architectural Review* May 1924, pages 180–85
Fully illustrated appraisal of Liberty's 'Elizabethan Inn' style of building in the new shop then underway behind Regent Street

**Konody, P. G.** 'Keramischer Wandschmuck und Dekorierte Mobel von W. J. Neatby' *Kunst und Kunsthandwerk* 6, 1903, pages 362–74
Contains the report of a Muthesius-type German art spy in Harrods' newly-opened Meat Hall

**Kulka, Heinrich** *Adolf Loos: das Werk des Architekten* Vienna 1931

*Moderne Ladenbauten: Aussen-und Innenarchitektur* Ernst Pollak Verlag, Berlin 1928
Although photographic reproduction is in the main poor, this picture book gives a good idea of the interiors of some very eclectic shops and cafés in Germany during the 1920s

**Moussinac, L.** *Robert Mallet-Stevens* Paris 1931

**Perry, Trevor** *Modern Shop-Front Construction* London 1933

**Poulain, Roger** *Boutiques* Vincent Fréal et Cie: Paris 1931

**Pound, Reginald** *Selfridge: A Biography* London 1960

**Priestland, Gerald** *Frying Tonight* London 1972
Devoted to the development and design of the British fish and chip shop

**Reilly, Charles** 'The Modern Store' *The Architectural Review* June 1935, pages 217–19
Illustrated with a series of drawings and photographs of traditional British stores, this article unfavourably compares them with Mendelsohn's Schocken store, Chemnitz

**Reilly, Charles, H.** 'Shop-fronts' *The Architectural Review* July 1935, pages 25–27

**Schoenbaum, David** *Hitler's Social Revolution: Class and Status in Nazi Germany 1933–39* London 1967
Contains some information on the Nazi 'cultural' hostility to department stores which culminated in the burning of 29 Jewish-owned stores in 1938. A useful social background to the exile of such eminent German architects as Erich Mendelsohn

'Shopping Streets Under Roofs of Glass' *Architectural Forum* January-February 1966, Vol. 124, pages 68–75
Illustrates the interior of Pomerantsev's GUM, Moscow, together with a variety of mid-19th century European shopping arcades. For the history and design of the great Milanese shopping arcade see also: Reed, Penelope 'Galleria Milan' *The Architectural Review* November 1966, pages 373–75

**Stedman, Spedan** 'The Layout and Design of Departmental Store Fittings in Relation to Their Uses' *Journal of the Royal Institute of British Architects* 5 September 1936

*Stores of the World Directory* Newman Books Ltd., London
A regularly revised trade directory which can provide useful names and addresses for shopping historians who wish to contact department stores directly for source material

**Taut, Bruno** *Modern Architecture* London 1929
Besides Schinkel's design for a proto-type department store, this important book also illustrates a rarely seen shop by Rietveld and a little Parisian fruit shop by Djo-Bourgeois

**Uhry, E.** 'Agrandissements des Magasins de la Samaritaine' *L'Architecte* II, 1907
Illustrates the great French *Art Nouveau* department store opened in 1905

**Westwood, Bryan** and **Westwood, Norman** *Smaller Retail Shops* London 1937

**Whittick, Arnold** *European Architecture in the 20th Century* London 1974
Contains one chapter, well illustrated with plans and photographs, which is specifically devoted to the department store as a modern building type

**Windsor, Alan** 'Michelin in Kensington' *The Architectural Review* October 1967, pages 309–10
Principally on the design of the Edwardian ceramic decoration in the Michelin car showrooms, Fulham Road, London

**Zola, Émile** *Au Bonheur des Dames* Paris 1883; translated by April Fitzlyon as *Ladies' Delight* John Calder Ltd: London 1957; issued as a paperback by Paul Elek Ltd: London 1960
Brilliant fictional account of the rise of a late 19th-century Parisian department store which contains many detailed descriptive passages of revolutionary display techniques